Thank Heaven for
Cats

•and other little pleasures•

Written and compiled by Carol Smith.

ISBN 978-1-60260-745-3

Published by Barbour Publishing, Inc., P.O. Box 719, Uhrichsville, Ohio 44683, www.barbourbooks.com

Our mission is to publish and distribute inspirational products offering exceptional value and biblical encouragement to the masses.

Member of the
Evangelical Christian
Publishers Association

Printed in India.

Thank Heaven for
Cats

• and other little pleasures •

BARBOUR
PUBLISHING

It's All Love

The reasons we share our lives with our cats may be different, and yet somehow they are tied by a common thread. It is love that links us together: love of the animals and their love for us, for reasons known only to them, but it's all the same. It's all love.

—SARA WILSON

If You Have a Cat

If you have a cat, congratulations. You have a relationship in which you are unconditionally loved, endlessly forgiven for your mistakes, never judged, and constantly entertained. A cat can make the stresses of your day disappear just by curling up in your lap at night.

—PAM JOHNSON-BENNETT

Keep It Simple

Never again will I make the simple into the complex. Something of true value does not become more valuable because it becomes complicated. Experience and conditions come and go; complications arise and fall away, but the simple action of God is eternal in the universe.

—DONALD CURTIS

Looking for Loopholes

Cats, no less liquid than their shadows
Offer no angles to the wind.
They slip, diminished, neat, through loopholes
Less than themselves. . .

—A.S.J. TESSIMOND

A Time for Petting

If there was any petting to be done, however, he chose to do it. Often he would sit looking at me, and then, moved by a delicate affection, come and pull at my coat and sleeve until he could touch my face with his nose, and then go away contented.

—CHARLES DUDLEY WARNER

The Last-Minute Leap

A cat can maintain a position of curled up somnolence on your knee until you are nearly upright. To the last minute she hopes your conscience will get the better of you and you will settle down again.

—PAM BROWN

Go Confidently

Go confidently in the direction of your dreams!
Live the life you've imagined. As you simplify
your life, the laws of the universe will be simpler.

—HENRY DAVID THOREAU

Nomad Skylights

She loves the gentle feel
Of sunbeams on her fur,
But as the day wears on,
It gives her cause to stir.

The sun's a fickle lover
Courted in ritual,
By my nomad cat under skylights,
Unable to sit still.

—CHARLES ALBANO

A Cat on Humans

Humans: No fur, no paws, no tail. They run away from mice. They never get enough sleep. How can you help but love such an absurd animal?

—AN ANONYMOUS CAT
ON HOMO SAPIENS

Curiosity

Seize the moment of excited curiosity on any
subject to solve your doubts; for if you let it pass,
the desire may never return, and you may remain
in ignorance.

—WILLIAM WIRT

My Ideal Cat

You remember my ideal cat has always a huge rat in its mouth, just going out of sight—though going out of sight in itself has a peculiar pleasure.

—EMILY DICKINSON

Free Souls

The really great thing about cats is their endless variety. One can pick a cat to fit almost any kind of decor, color, scheme, income, personality, mood. But under the fur, whatever color it may be, there still lies, essentially unchanged, one of the world's free souls.

—ERIC GURNEY

Simplicity and Peace

When we have reached this total deprivation, what shall we do? Abide in simplicity and peace, as Job on his ash heap, repeating, "Blessed are the poor in spirit; those who have nothing have all, since they have God."

—JEAN-PIERRE DE CAUSSADE

My Cat the Clown

My cat the clown: paying no mind to whom he should impress. Merely living his life, doing what pleases him, and making me smile.

—ANONYMOUS

Complete Relaxation

Who among us hasn't envied a cat's ability
to ignore the cares of daily life and to relax
completely?

—KAREN BRADEMEYER

Lapping Up the Warmth

If a dog jumps up into your lap, it is because he is fond of you; but if a cat does the same thing, it is because your lap is warmer.

—ALFRED NORTH WHITEHEAD

Purr-fection Purr-sonified

The cat has been described as the most perfect animal, the acme of muscular perfection and the supreme example in the animal kingdom of the coordination of mind and muscle.

—ROSEANNE AMBROSE BROWN

Petting the Tiger

As every cat owner knows, nobody owns a cat.

—ELLEN PERRY BERKELEY

Life Is Good

There's no other sound like a purr, right by
your ear as you are waking up. The slow lull of
contentment. The paw half over the face. The
seemingly effortless drone that announces to
anyone close enough to hear, "Life is good."

Of All God's Creatures

Of all God's creatures, there is only one that cannot be made slave of the leash. That one is the cat. If man could be crossed with the cat it would improve the man, but it would deteriorate the cat.

—MARK TWAIN

Admiration and Envy

I think one reason we admire cats, those of us who do, is their proficiency in one-upmanship. They always seem to come out on top, no matter what they are doing—or pretend they do. Rarely do you see a cat discomfited. They have no conscience, and they never regret. Maybe we secretly envy them.

—BARBARA WEBSTER

The Patience of a Cat

As anyone who has ever been around a cat for any length of time well knows, cats have enormous patience with the limitations of the human mind.

—CLEVELAND AMORY

Gratitude Begets Gratitude

The more we express our gratitude to God for our blessings, the more he will bring to our mind other blessings. The more we are aware of to be grateful for, the happier we become.

—EZRA TAFT BENSON

Just Try Not to Smile

It is impossible to keep a straight face in the presence of one or more kittens.

—CYNTHIA E. VARNADO

The Language of Love

French novelist Colette was a firm cat-lover. When she was in the U.S. she saw a cat sitting in the street. She went over to talk to it and the two of them mewed at each other for a friendly minute. Colette turned to her companion and exclaimed, *"Enfin! Quelqu'un qui parle francais."* (At last! Someone who speaks French!)

—ANONYMOUS

Friends as Pets

You don't get to pick your own nickname.
They've gotta give you one. It's like we're all tryin'
to make pets out of each other and we're not
comfortable unless we get to name 'em.

—LAURA MONCUR

No Harm in Asking

Cats seem to go on the principal that it never does any harm to ask for what you want.

—JOSEPH WOOD KRUTCH

Cats of Mine

Companions elusive at times invasive at others
not wanting to be bothered except to further their
own agendas; a place to sleep, food, occasional
warmth and attention. Small furry people they
seem to be in their selfishness but smarter because
nothing is expected.

—BESS KEMP

The Feline Invitation

Few things bring out the passion in people like cats. Many humans adore felines as they adore no other creature. There is an intimacy to cats— a club only they can invite you to join. It is the feeling that I am a trusted and special friend, fully sanctioned to enter a private world.

—SARA WILSON

Blue Eyes

He came into my life with eyes so blue I named him Frank, for Frank Sinatra. Those eyes saw me through a move, and the loss of a love, and the refinding of myself. And I buried him with daisies and was so grateful that I had been his.

Appreciation of the Fundamental Things

The more one does and sees and feels,
the more one is able to do, and the more genuine
may be one's appreciation of fundamental
things like home, and love, and understanding
companionship.

—AMELIA EARHART

My Cat Has Got No Name

My cat has got no name
We simply call him Cat;
He doesn't seem to blame
Anyone for that.

For he is not like us
Who often, I'm afraid,
Kick up quite a fuss
If our names are mislaid.

—VERNON SCANNELL

Pass Your Time Enjoyably

Life is a matter of passing the time enjoyably.
There may be other things in life, but I've been
too busy passing my time enjoyably to think very
deeply about them.

—PETER COOK

Flexible Kitten

A kitten is so flexible that she is almost double;
the hind parts are equivalent to another kitten
with which the forepart plays. She does not
discover that her tail belongs to her until you tread
on it.

—HENRY DAVID THOREAU

The Presence of a Cat

There is something about the presence of a cat. . .
that seems to take the bite out of being alone.

—LOUIS J. CAMUTI

The Plight of the Cat

Like annoying women who marry a man and
then instantly want to reform him, cats have very
firm ideas about what they want in a lifetime
companion. . . . After all, they didn't choose you,
they got stuck with you. Like mail-order brides,
if they had hissed and spat and refused to be
carried over the threshold, who knows what would
have become of them?

—INGRID NEWKIRK

Staying Close

This morning I woke with my feline companion by my side, and I gave her a good head scratch to start off the day. Then as I drew my hand away her paws curled around it as if to say, "Just stay close for a moment more."

The Good Life

She's adept at sleeping on either of her sides
Her right when she's up against him and her left when
She's up against her
She likes to keep them happy this way
The only drawback to the nightly bliss
Is that he occasionally snores abruptly and wickedly
And this can truly rev up the old kitty ticker for a bit.

—WALT AND BONNIE PHILLIPS

What Brings You Joy?

What little things bring you joy? They are different for each of us. . . .when I really feel listened to. . . when my son gives me a big hug and holds on tight. . . Make your own list—and then be sure to indulge regularly.

—SUSANNAH SETON

A Cat Named April

When I was a small girl, I had a cat named April.
April had a litter box, litter, food dishes, food,
and water. Now I realize how deprived she
was! Today's felines have condos, trees, towers,
hammocks, cradles, playhouses, and tunnels.
Some even have cat-sized sofas, chairs, and beds.
Yet April loved me well, even in her poverty.

Grown Cats at Play

There is nothing in the animal world, to my mind, more delightful than grown cats at play. They are so swift and light and graceful, so subtle and designing, and yet so richly comic.

—MONICA EDWARDS

A Good Head Rub

There's nothing more enjoyable than a good head rub for the kitten of the house. He rolls and lolls and pulls my hand closer with his paws until his ears are scratched and his face is rubbed and he's ready for another nap.

Play

The real joy of life is in its play. Play is anything we do for the joy and love of doing it, apart from any profit, compulsion, or sense of duty. It is the real joy of living.

—WALTER RAUSCHBUSCH

The Calming Effect

There has never been a cat
Who couldn't calm me down
By walking slowly
Past my chair.

—ROD MCKUEN

Double the Contentment

Four little Persians, but only one looked in my direction. I extended a tentative finger and two soft paws clung to it. There was a contented sound of purring, I suspect on both our parts.

—GEORGE FREEDLEY

The Finesse of the Feline

As if expecting visitors, your cat is always up in the morning, looking well rested, washed, and groomed. At mealtimes, you never have to shout, "For the umpteenth time, will you come and eat?" Cats are fastidious about their litter boxes. They try to keep their claws filed down, and they never snore.

—INGRID NEWKIRK

A Tabby Moment

A tan tabby, with the softest of lines etched in fur
that any teddy bear would envy, sits on my lap with
a purr of contentment, and I dare not move.
It's not so much the cat that I hesitate to disturb as
the moment.

Communication

Why does the human need so much material
translated into so many different languages
When obviously the cat understands them all?
Isn't language merely the means by which we
communicate our thought pictures and ideas?
Since the cat can understand all of them, is she
not reading our very souls?

—DUTCH CARRIE

No Surprise

According to a recent poll of the worldwide cat population, the average feline does indeed feel superior to its human "owners." In fact, 53 percent of cats, spanning a range of species, expressed a strong belief that they would one day control the world.

Horizontal Thinking

We spend most of our time and energy in a kind of horizontal thinking. We move along the surface of things [but] there are times when we stop.
We sit still. We lose ourselves in a pile of leaves or its memory. We listen and breezes from a whole other world begin to whisper.

—JAMES CARROLL

My Cat Sassafras

My cat Sassafras watches me each morning as I get ready for the day. I have to wonder what she thinks about these human rituals in which we apply our supposed beauty rather than simply wearing it upon our waking as she does.

Cat of the Streets

I want to create a cat like the real cats I see crossing the streets, not like those you see in houses. They have nothing in common. The cat of the streets has bristling fur. It runs like a fiend, and if it looks at you, you think it is going to jump in your face.

—PABLO PICASSO

Happy People

Happy people roll with the punches. They know from experience that everything changes. Today's good fortune may vanish tomorrow; today's crises may turn out to be tomorrow's good fortune. It's always better to wait and see before you decide the story has been written.

—UNKNOWN

A Cat Never Barks

Your cat will never threaten your popularity by barking at three in the morning. He won't attack the mailman or eat the drapes, although he may climb the drapes to see how the room looks from the ceiling.

—HELEN POWERS

Free Entertainment

I have noticed that what cats most appreciate in a human being is not the ability to produce food, which they take for granted—but his or her entertainment value.

—GEOFFREY HOUSEHOLD

The Strength of Companionship

Two people are better off than one, for they can help each other succeed. If one person falls, the other can reach out and help. But someone who falls alone is in real trouble. Likewise, two people lying close together can keep each other warm. But how can one be warm alone?

—ECCLESIASTES 4:9–11 NLT

Easy to Entertain

She found a ribbon in an obscure spot down the hall and for hours she tossed and chased and tossed and chased. Then, finally exhausted, she left it beside the shelf to be discovered on another day as if for the first time.

Tranquility

Oh loving puss, come hither and purr
Let me stroke your soft, warm fur.
Let me gaze into your loving eyes
How great their depth. . .how very wise.

What comfort your dear presence brings
I forget all sad, unhappy things.
Let no man live without this peace
Proof that God's wonders never cease.

—DUTCH CARRIE

The Souls of Animals

If having a soul means being able to feel love and loyalty and gratitude, then animals are better off than a lot of humans.

—JAMES HERRIOT

Peace

There is no need to go to India or anywhere else to find peace. You will find that deep place of silence right in your room, your garden, or even your bathtub.

—ELISABETH KUBLER-ROSS

Ode to Catnip

Oh, catnip! What intoxicating appeal
Doth this herbaceous perennial impart!
In loving homes I chase this madcap plant;
While families gather, laughing.
I love to raise a fuss.

—WILLIAM SHAKESPAW

Feline Insomniacs?

Cats are rather delicate creatures and they are subject to a good many ailments, but I never heard of one who suffered from insomnia.

—JOSEPH WOOD KRUTCH

Live Wholeheartedly

Live wholeheartedly. Be surprised!
Give thanks and praise!
Then you will discover the fullness of your life.

—BROTHER DAVID STEINDL RASE

Twenty Minutes Early

Cats do care. For example they know instinctively what time we have to be at work in the morning and they wake us up twenty minutes before the alarm goes off.

—MICHAEL NELSON

A Hairball in My Heart

He swings from the chandelier, he paws my peanut butter, and he knocks over my drink in the most unfortunate places in the house—but I still love him like crazy. It's like a hairball in my heart.

—AUDRA FOVEO-ALBA

My Cat Comes to Be with Me

My cat may not love me as I love him.
He may not crave my approval.
He may not buy me toys and treats.
He may not take me to the doctor.
But he comes into the room when I sit down
to be with me in the quiet of the day.
Sometimes I think he loves me far better.

Feline Snowball

I woke up this morning to the sound of two cats entwined in a roly-poly play fight making their snowball way down the hall until they separated only to chase each other back around and start all over again. And I have to admit, I wished I could be a part of the gymnastics.

The Cat of Cats

I am the cat of cats. I am
The everlasting cat!
Cunning and old, and sleek as jam,
The everlasting cat!
I hunt the vermin in the night—
The everlasting cat!
For I see best without the light—
The everlasting cat!

—WILLIAM BRIGHTY RANDS

A Breed unto Herself

You should have seen her. Cutest little pixie face with big beautiful eyes. . .a cute little turned-up nose. . .luxurious curly hair. . .and big old ears that would put Spock to shame. Needless to say, I was smitten.

Where Cats Gather

Often cats are talked about as aloof and difficult and standoffish, but I have found them to be quite the opposite. Wherever I sit down, they gather. They invite me in. They spend their time with me. They show their own kind of love. And I wouldn't trade it for anything.

Expressions of Love

James Herriot, the beloved veterinarian, enjoyed the company of cats from the time he was a small boy. He stated, "Their innate grace and daintiness and their deeply responsive affection made them all dear to me. . . . I have felt cats rubbing their faces against mine and touching my cheek with claws carefully sheathed. These things, to me, are expressions of love."

A Cat's Advice

More than likely it was the cat who first coined
and put into practice the sage advice: "If you would
have a thing done well, you must do it yourself."

—LAWRENCE N. JOHNSON

Friendship

Friendship is the source of the greatest pleasures, and without friends even the most agreeable pursuits become tedious.

—SAINT THOMAS AQUINAS

Who's the Pastime?

When I play with my cat, who knows if I am not a
pastime to her more than she is to me? . . .
Who knows but that she pities me for being no
wiser than to play with her; and laughs,
and censures my folly in making sport for her,
when we two play together.

—MICHEL DE MONTAIGNE

Leonardo Should Know

The smallest feline is a masterpiece.

—LEONARDO DA VINCI

Really Living

There isn't much better in this life than finding a way to spend a few hours in conversation with people you respect and love. You have to carve this time out of your life, because you aren't really living without it.

—ANONYMOUS

A Cat on Bug

Nothing can prowl and pounce like a cat on a bug.
Seriously slinking through the grass, at once Red
Baron and the serpent of Eden. Then suddenly
a lion on the attack. And who cares whether the
insect is even caught; it's the hunt that returns him
to the jungle.

A Mother Cat's Purr

Sleep the half-sleep, Kittens dear,
While your mother
Cat-naps near.
Every kitten
Is a cat
And you must
Remember that
Naps for cats
Are mostly fake:
Any time
Is time to wake,
Or time to pounce,
Or time to scat.
That's what sleep is—
For a cat.

—JANE YOLEN

Ol' Tom

Tom was. . .well, Tom was just Tom. What you saw was what you got. No pretenses, no posing, no talking about his background or his hired help or what he'd eaten that day for lunch. Tom was just a big old fun-loving street cat of uncertain parentage, a cat who radiated love like a discarded can of mackerel radiates. . .well, something that's very difficult to describe.

A "Tail" of Exclamation

I never tire of watching my kitty's tail whether it's swishing or swaying or simply standing at attention as he wanders 'bout the room. It is not only his appendage, but also his punctuation—sometimes an exclamation point of sorts—but always an indicator of his moods.

Wild Kitty

When I was small, I made the acquaintance of a
cat named Wild Kitty. She lived up to her name,
for her home was in the woods and she could be
touched by no one. As a lonely little girl,
I patiently coaxed her with tidbits of food.
One spring day, she came to me, and allowed me
to befriend her. Later that year, she honored me by
depositing her kittens on my porch.

The Fastidious Feline

Just as the would-be debutante will fret and fuss over every detail till all is perfect, so will the fastidious feline patiently toil until every whiskertip is in place.

—LYNN HOLLYN

The Sweetness of Friendship

In the sweetness of friendship; let there be laughter and sharing of pleasures. For in the dew of little things the heart finds its morning and is refreshed.

—KAHLIL GIBRAN

Places to Look

Places to look: behind the books in the bookshelf,
any cupboard with a gap too small for any cat to
squeeze through, the top of anything sheer,
under anything too low for a cat to squash under
and inside the piano.

—ROSEANNE AMBROSE-BROWN

Pet-able Art

There's no need for a piece of sculpture in a home that has a cat.

—WESLEY BATES

When the Puppies Came

My cats were appalled when the puppies came
They spat and they howled at such gangly arrivals.
Yet they have forgiven the pups and me
With time and enough naps taken together.

Firefly Ballet

Kittens chase fireflies through the grass like a ballet of sorts, leaping and flipping completely unself-aware of the incredibly difficult feats that they, in their passion, commit to with abandon. It's the joy of the chase they seem to feel, and that alone.

Cat Lying Down

When my cat lies down, it is with utmost gravity.

No circular trampling first like a clumsy canine,
no great sigh like a human being on a couch.

My cat lies down slowly, naturally, smoothly,
participating with controlled abandon in a
dignified gravitational event.

—ALAN HARRIS

Defining a Kitten

Kittens. What can you say about kittens that hasn't already been said? Kittens are furry and funny and funky and fuzzy and frenetic and filled with the promise of a fantastical future. They leave you frazzled and flustered and frantically flitting yet flirty and full of festivity.

Egostical, Irresponsible, Suave, and Delightful

The great charm of cats is their rampant egotism, their devil-may-care attitude toward responsibility, their disinclination to earn an honest dollar. In a continent which screams neurotically about cooperation and the Golden Rule, cats are disdainful of everything but their own immediate interests and they contrive to be so suave and delightful about it that they even receive the apotheosis of a National Cat Week.

—ROBERTSON DAVIES

Living with the Animals

I think I could turn and live with animals, they are so placid and self-contained, I stand and look at them long and long.

—WALT WHITMAN

Learning to Get Along

When I raise a cat from kittenhood, it learns to read me so well that it can con me and predict what I'm going to do. A young adult cat doesn't know what to expect from me and I don't know what to expect from it, so we immediately have each other's attention.

—KARL LEWIS MILLER

The Pleasure of Conversation

Talk is by far the most accessible of pleasures.
It costs nothing in money, it is all profit,
it completes our education, founds and fosters our
friendships, and can be enjoyed at any age and in
almost any state of health.

—ROBERT LOUIS STEVENSON

A Pull towards the Human

If the pull of the outside world is strong,
there is also a pull towards the human. The cat
may disappear on its own errands, but sooner or
later, it returns once again for a little while,
to greet us with its own type of love.

—LLOYD ALEXANDER

Unforgettable

To anyone who has ever been owned by a cat,
it will come as no surprise that there are all sorts
of things about your cat you will never, as long as
you live, forget. Not the least of these is your first
sight of him or her.

—CLEVELAND AMORY

I'd Like to Think

I'd like to think I owned the cat,
  that condescends to share my flat,
I give him all of my rationed food,
  and cater to his every mood,
I'd like to think he'd go to seed,
  if I weren't there to meet his every need,
And yet the fact is plain to see,
  That doggone cat, owns me!

—VANESSA ROGERSON

The Command of the Claw

There is a kind of respect that even the smallest of claws commands. One swat of a kitty cat's paw and a hundred-pound dog jumps back to save his nose from a shredding. All because of a little claw attached to a little paw attached to a face that would melt the coldest heart.

A Few Common Characteristics

It would be hard indeed to list all the fascinating qualities attributed to cats over the ages— especially since every cat seems to have a unique temperament. Nevertheless, most cats share a few common characteristics. . .dignity, complexity, empathy, grace, presence, cleanliness, and charm.

—ERIC SWANSON

If I Were a Cat

If I were a cat
An essay. By me.
If I were a cat. . .I'd loll about. . .roll about. . .
stroll about. . .
Doing catlike things.
If I were a cat. . .wait a minute.
I AM a cat.

Fulfilled Expectations

Unlike us, cats never outgrow their delight in cat capacities, nor do they settle finally for limitations. Cats, I think, live out their lives fulfilling their expectations.

—IRVING TOWNSEND

The Mystery of the Grocery

Ever consider what pets must think of us? I mean, here we come back from a grocery store with the most amazing haul—chicken, pork, half a cow. They must think we're the greatest hunters on earth!

—ANNE TYLER

Sleep and Let Sleep

He seems the incarnation of everything soft and silky and velvety, without a sharp edge in his composition, a dreamer whose philosophy is sleep and let sleep.

—SAKI

When from Our Better Selves

When from our better selves we have too long been parted by the hurrying world, and droop. Sick of its business, of its pleasures tired, how gracious, how benign in solitude.

—WILLIAM WORDSWORTH

The Ideal of Calm

The ideal of calm exists in a sitting cat.

—JULES REYNARD

Noisy Velcro

I think my favorite thing in the house has to be the cat. . .mainly because she's just like a big piece of noisy Velcro when you toss her at the sofa.

—MICHELLE ARGABRITE

The Dignity of Felines

The dignity of felines is unrivaled. From their
baths to their naps, they approach every aspect of
life with the manners of a Southern belle,
the intelligence of a Nobel prize-winner,
and depth of thought of a shaman.

Let Go

If a man insisted always on being serious, and never allowed himself a bit of fun and relaxation, he would go mad or become unstable without knowing it.

—HERODOTUS

Just to Make Sure
You're There

Even the shiest cat craves her owner's affection.
While you're busy typing away or engrossed in a
video, she may just crawl out from her hiding place
under the bed and touch her nose to your bare
foot or rub her whiskers against your shin—just to
make sure you're there.

—ERIC SWANSON

Why Do They Do It?

Cats grace us with their affection.... When they curl up on your lap, it's because they think you're worth spending time with. When they climb onto your shoulder, it's because they trust that you will carry them safely. When they lie across your magazine, it's because they can't believe their best friend would rather look at this flat, boring thing than their sleek, gorgeous, purring selves.

—BRIAN KILCOMMONS
AND SARA WILSON

The Birth of a Kitten

The birth of a kitten is one of the most moving events you can see. New life offers an opportunity to enjoy innocence, trust, and love generously given.

—MORDECAI SIEGAL

My Cat in Her Wanderings

Balancing, teetering, seemingly never afraid of the fall from the fence or the rail or the highest cabinet in the kitchen. Slight of step and nimble beyond imagination, weaving between the precious items on the bureau but not displacing one. No circus act holds such suspense and grace as my cat in her wanderings.

Whose Pet?

I rarely meddled in the cat's personal affairs and she rarely meddled in mine. Neither of us was foolish enough to attribute human emotions to our pets.

—KINKY FRIEDMAN

One Happy Moment

Who will tell whether one happy moment of love or the joy of breathing or walking on a bright morning and smelling the fresh air, is not worth all the suffering and effort which life implies.

—ERICH FROMM

It's All for the Cat's Sake

Everything that moves, serves to interest and amuse a cat. He is convinced that nature is busying herself with his diversion; he can conceive of no other purpose in the universe.

—F. A. PARADIS DE MONCRIF

Different Ways of Showing Love

A dog will show his love by jumping on you at the front door. A cat will show his love by ignoring you, and then curling up next to you when you need it most.

—DANIELLE ASSON

Dreams That Have No End

Drowsing, they take the noble attitude of a great sphinx, who, in a desert land, sleeps always, dreaming dreams that have no end.

—CHARLES BAUDELAIRE

Tiberius the Cat?

Cruel, but composed and bland,
Dumb, inscrutable and grand,
So Tiberius might have sat,
Had Tiberius been a cat.

—MATTHEW ARNOLD

Noah's Ark
(Feline Wing)

Tigers. Tabbies. Manxes and mountain lions. Persians and panthers and pumas. That regally-maned Leo Lion and his svelte, charming wife, Leonora. Shorthairs and longhairs and no-hairs, all in pairs. You never heard such meowing and purring and hissing and growling and roaring, never saw such a richly diverse concentration of aloof, aggressive, frolicsome, and occasionally haughty behavior. It was simply wonderful!

Calico Callie

You know those moments you get sometimes when suddenly just the slightest bit of self-doubt creeps into the picture and you can't help but wonder how accurate your own worldview is, and you start questioning your purpose and maybe thinking, "You know, it's possible that the world doesn't revolve around me"? Well, this calico NEVER had moments like that.

I Can't Resist a Cat

I simply can't resist a cat, particularly a purring one. They are the cleanest, cunningest, and most intelligent things I know, outside of the girl you love, of course.

—MARK TWAIN

Expressing Himself

Of all domestic animals the cat is the most expressive. His face is capable of showing a wide range of expressions. His tail is a mirror of his mind. His gracefulness is surpassed only by his agility. And, along with all these, he has a sense of humor.

—WALTER CHANDOHA

You Belong to Me

When your cat rubs the side of its face along your leg, it's affectionately marking you with its scent, identifying you as its private property, saying, in effect, "You belong to me."

—SUSAN MCDONOUGH, D.M.V.

Looking for Happiness

You will never be happy if you continue to search for what happiness consists of. You will never live if you are looking for the meaning of life.

—ALBERT CAMUS

What Greater Gift?

What greater gift than the love of a cat?

—CHARLES DICKENS

Peaceful Sleep

Many are asking, "Who can show us any good?"
Let the light of your face shine upon us, O LORD.
You have filled my heart with greater joy than when
their grain and new wine abound.
I will lie down and sleep in peace, for you alone,
O LORD, make me dwell in safety.

—PSALM 4:6–8 NIV

Make Me Laugh

Among those whom I like or admire, I can find no common denominator, but among those whom I love, I can: all of them make me laugh.

—W. H. AUDEN

Have You Given Much Thought to a Whisker?

Have you given much thought to a whisker?
It warns its wearer of tight little places.
It proffers delight from most feline faces.
It has such a function and form,
For all those on whom it is worn.

You Are Her Everything

As far as your cat's concerned, you are Mommy,
Daddy, God, Best Friend, and Sibling all rolled
into one; and if she sometimes seems annoyed with
you, just remember how long you spent in therapy
trying to deal with your feelings about important
figures in your life.

—ERIC SWANSON

The Score
(Trash Talk Included)

The scoreboard doesn't lie. Six hundred million cats in the world, a measly four hundred million dogs. Folks, that's a decisive victory. . .a rout. . .a good old-fashioned rump-kicking! Sorry, dogs, but let's just see you slobbering, oh-so-eager-to-please beasties try to catch up. Woo-hoo! Cats rule, dogs drool!

Just an Old Cat

Just an old cat
That sits by the door
And looks up at me when I enter
Just an old cat
That lies on the floor
And softly meows when I leave
Just an old cat
That bats at the air
And catches my shoes as I walk by
Just an old cat
But wishes be told
I'd wish for him never to leave.

Tufts and Tufts
of the Softest Fur

It's the season of shedding, when a simple hand stroke down the back of my tabby leaves me as fur-filled as he. Tufts and tufts of the softest fur as the winter coat gives way to the sleeker summer 'do.

Jungle Instinct?

Is it yet another survival of jungle instinct,
this hiding away from prying eyes at important
times? Or merely a gesture of independence, a
challenge to man and his stupid ways?

—MICHAEL JOSEPH

Growing Friendship

A friendship can weather most things and thrive in thin soil; but it needs a little mulch of letters and phone calls and small, silly presents every so often—just to save it from drying out completely.

—PAM BROWN

Winning Over a Cat

Before a cat will condescend
To treat you as a trusted friend,
Some little token of esteem
Is needed, like a dish of cream.

—T. S. ELIOT

The Meat Loaf Position

Surely the cat, when it assumes the meat loaf position and gazes meditatively through slitted eyes, is pondering thoughts of utter profundity.

—MIJ COLSON BARNUM

Have You Given Much Thought to a Purr?

Have you given much thought to a purr?
The grating, half-growling,
Much different from howling,
Delight in the form of a whirr.
Have you given much thought to a purr?

Peaches

Peaches was a kitty who loved to chase squirrels. Therefore, her owners were shocked when a very pregnant Peaches adopted an abandoned baby squirrel. When she gave birth to her kittens, she placed the baby squirrel with her brood and nursed them together!

—ALLAN ZULLO AND
MARA BOVSUN

Gratitude

We tend to forget that happiness doesn't come as a result of getting something we don't have, but rather of recognizing and appreciating what we do have.

—FREDERICK KEONIG

Perfect Day

Sunlight gently tickling the whiskers first thing
this morning. A languid stroll around the
premises. Nap. Toying with the chipmunk from
the garden. Two kinds of fish for lunch. Nap.
An awesome ball of yarn that somehow managed
to fill three rooms. Catnip. (Actually, the catnip
preceded the yarn.) Nap. A mouse or two, and that
misfortunate bird. There was other stuff, too, but
those are the highlights.

Cat or Human?

In many ways I behave toward my cats as if they were human—and I'm not alone in that. Similarly, to my cats I am some sort of cat. We are all a bit confused on the overlap between people and cats.

—ROGER TABOR

It's Not a Cat. It's. . .

A small, four-legged, fur-bearing extortionist.
A wildlife control expert impersonator.
An unprogrammable animal.
A four footed allergen.
A hair relocation expert.
A treat-seeking missile.
A lapwarmer with a built-in buzzer.
A small, furry lap fungus.

—GANDEE VASAN

Cats Are Practical

The cat does not offer services. The cat offers itself. Of course he wants care and shelter. You don't buy love for nothing. Like all pure creatures, cats are practical.

—WILLIAM S. BURROUGHS

Lewis on Friendship

Friendship is unnecessary, like philosophy, like art, like the universe itself (for God did not need to create). It has no survival value; rather it is one of those things which give value to survival.

—C. S. LEWIS

Telegraph, Tell-a-Cat

You see, wire telegraph is a kind of a very,
very long cat. You pull his tail in New York and
his head is meowing in Los Angeles. Do you
understand this? And radio operates exactly the
same way: you send signals here, they receive them
there. The only difference is that there is no cat.

—ALBERT EINSTEIN

Happiness Is Like a Cat

Happiness is like a cat. If you try to coax it or call it, it will avoid you. It will never come. But if you pay no attention to it and go about your business, you'll find it rubbing up against your legs and jumping into your lap.

—WILLIAM BENNETT

Bird Watching

Cats MUST have comfy places to sit and look out. To the dedicated bird-watcher, nothing makes the time pass quicker, and the whiskers twitch faster, than the object of her natural, abiding interest and careful study.

—INGRID NEWKIRK

I Picked Out a Kitten

I picked out a kitten
The smallest of all
Runt of the litter, yet belle of the ball.
I picked out a kitten
The loudest by far.
I wrapped her up tightly, and off to the car.
I picked out a kitten
And whisked her away
And home became homier still on that day.

What Does Your Cat Want?

Sometimes all they want is some special sign of affection. For instance, Pumpkin's dish may be full, you may have scratched her behind the ears until your hand is ready to fall off, but she keeps right on giving you a round, insistent stare or meowing her fool head off.

—ERIC SWANSON

Real Silence

Not merely an absence of noise, Real Silence begins when a reasonable being withdraws from the noise in order to find peace and order in his inner sanctuary.

—PETER MINARD

Cat Burglars

Little Kitten Caboodle was home alone,
working on her calligraphy, when the thugs broke
in through the third-floor skylight. It was the
notorious Katt Brothers, a pair of bad-news kitties
who were born mean and grew nastier with each
passing year. They cleaned the place out:
the high-end home entertainment center, the
entire contents of the fully stocked tuna cellar,
the fine art collection, even Caboodle's easel and
blank canvases. In fact, those heartless burglars
took everything but the kitten's ink.

A Proud Spirit

All cats are possessed of a proud spirit, and the surest way to forfeit the esteem of a cat is to treat him as an inferior being.

—MICHAEL JOSEPH

Show a Little Appreciation

A cat can be trusted to purr when she is pleased,
which is more than can be said for human beings.

—WILLIAM RALPH INGE

Learn the Meaning of Friendship

Friendship is the hardest thing in the world to explain. It's not something you learn in school. But if you haven't learned the meaning of friendship, you really haven't learned anything.

—MUHAMMAD ALI

Intercepted Footsteps

Cats have intercepted my footsteps at the ankle for so long that my gait, both at home and on tour, has been compared to that of a man wading through low surf.

—ROY BLOUNT, JR.

Intrepid Explorer

There is no more intrepid explorer than a kitten.
He makes perilous voyages into cellar and attic,
he scales the roofs of neighboring houses,
he thrusts his little inquiring nose into half-shut
doors. . .he gets himself into every kind of trouble,
and he's always sorry when it is too late.

Cats Upside Down

What a treat it is to see cats lie upside down and bump their rumps from side to side. I think it means they have just won the lottery. I always check in the cat bed for a winning stub.

—INGRID NEWKIRK

A Startled Cat

A startled cat is a bouncing exclamation mark,
moving his whole body at once, straight into the
air as if the world simply bounced him into the air.
Who does not catch his breath then laugh out loud
at the scene?

You're Okay, He's Okay

At times, cats seem like hairy little people.
In times of sickness or sorrow they may wrap
your head in their paws, nuzzle your neck, or lick
your cheek. A calm atmosphere is deeply linked
to survival. If you are upset or ill, your cat will do
whatever it takes to soothe you, so that his home
becomes secure once more.

—ERIC SWANSON

Cats I Have Known, Part One

My siblings, Felix and Winthrop and Penelope, were the first cats I really got to know, and the best siblings I cat could hope to have. Then there were the neighborhood toms, Simon and Sylvester and Muggsy and Stripes. And of course, poor Fido, who never quite got over the twisted name his folks laid on him.

My Many Cats

I've loved many a cat in my lifetime, and I've
grieved each when they said "so long."
And I'll love several more should I live long
enough, and be grateful long after they're gone.

Musical Kitty

The Italian composer Domenico Scarlatti gave his cat the credit for the composition of one of his sonatas. After a nap, Scarlatti heard his cat walking on the harpsichord. The musical phrase of the cat became a sonata known as "The Cat's Fugue."

—ALLEN ZULLO AND
MARA BOYSUN

A Kitten

He's nothing much but fur
And two round eyes of blue,
He has a giant purr
And a midget mew.

He darts and pats the air,
He starts and cocks his ear,
When there is nothing there
For him to see and hear. . . .

Then half-way through a leap
His startled eyeballs close,
And he drops off to sleep
With one paw on his nose.

—ELEANOR FARJEON

Those Who Rekindle the Inner Spirit

In everyone's life, at some time, our inner fire goes out. It is then burst into flame by an encounter with another human being. We should all be thankful for those people who rekindle the inner spirit.

—ALBERT SCHWEITZER

Lessons from My Cat

Everything I know I learned from my cat:
When you're hungry, eat. When you're tired,
nap in a sunbeam. When you go to the vet's,
pee on your owner.

—GARY SMITH

A High-Tech Device?

The cat is surprisingly similar to other high-tech devices you may already own. Like personal digital assistants, it is compact and portable. Like a home security system, it is capable of functioning autonomously for extended periods without direct human intervention. But *unlike* virtually any other product. . .it is, for the most part, self-cleaning.

—DAVID BRUNNER
AND SAM STALL

A Sufficient Contribution

The kitten has a luxurious, Bohemian, unpuritanical nature. It eats six meals a day, plays furiously with a toy mouse and a piece of rope, and suddenly falls into a deep sleep whenever the fit takes it. It never feels the necessity to do anything to justify its existence; it does not want to be a Good Citizen; it has never heard of Service. It knows that it is beautiful and delightful, and it considers that a sufficient contribution to the general good. And in return for its beauty and charm it expects fish, meat, and vegetables, a comfortable bed, a chair by the grate fire, and endless petting.

—ROBERTSON DAVIES

Kentucky's Story

His name was Kentucky, Tucker for short. He came to his own whistle, fetched a little feline-sized ball, and challenged any animal that entered the yard. A mix of cat and dog, but the best of both, he meowed only when he had something important to say. I will always remember him for that.

Fear of Cats

Fear of cats, termed *ailurophobia*, is as old as the
sun and has something to do with that ethereal
quality of cats that makes them so mysterious.
Even the way they look at a person can be a little
unnerving at times. There's something about that
fixed unblinking stare that gives the impression
that they are looking right into one's soul.

—DR. NICHOLAS DODMAN

Cat-a-holic

Le Mew read the word, said it aloud, pondered it. He had never heard of such a thing! But it somehow seemed plausible. After all, the old woman a couple of blocks over had something like seven cats, and she was always taking in another stray. Perhaps she was suffering from a feline addiction.

Foss

The popularizing of the cat by writers and artists such as Edward Lear and Beatrix Potter has made them endearing images for children's pets. Edward Lear was so devoted to his cat Foss that when he moved, his new villa was constructed exactly like his old house so as not to inconvenience his cat in any way!

—ROGER TABOR

The Advantage of the Animals

Animals have these advantages over man:
they never hear the clock strike, they die without
any idea of death, they have no theologians
to instruct them, their last moments are
not disturbed by unwelcome and unpleasant
ceremonies, their funerals cost them nothing,
and no one starts lawsuits over their wills.

—VOLTAIRE

Squatter's Rights

Listen, kitten,
Get this clear,
This is my chair.
I sit here.
Okay, kitty,
We can share;
When I'm not home,
It's your chair.
Listen cat
How about
If I use it
When you're out?

—RICHARD SHAW

Two Friends

Many a person has held close, throughout their
entire lives, two friends that always remained
strange to one another, because one of them
attracted by virtue of similarity, the other by
difference.

—EMIL LUDWIG

Who's Fussy?

A cat isn't fussy—just so long as you remember he likes his milk in the shallow, rose-patterned saucer and his fish on the blue plate. From which he will take it, and eat it off the floor.

—ARTHUR BRIDGES

Comfort

All praise to God, the Father of our Lord Jesus
Christ. God is our merciful Father and the source
of all comfort. He comforts us in all our troubles
so that we can comfort others. When they are
troubled, we will be able to give them the same
comfort God has given us.

—2 CORINTHIANS 1:3–4 NLT

Be My Friend

Don't walk behind me, I may not lead. Don't walk in front of me, I may not follow. Just walk beside me and be my friend.

—UNKNOWN

Our Lovely Cat

Oh gorgeous Celestino, for
God made lovely things, yet
Our lovely cat surpasses them all;
The gold, the iron, the waterfall,
The nut, the peach, apple, granite
Are lovely things to look at, yet,
Our lovely cat surpasses them all.

—JOHN GITTINGS
AGE 8, ENGLAND

What Your Cat Will Do for You

When you've been working too hard, a cat will walk across your papers to let you know it's time for a break. A cat will show his gratitude for the simplest act, such as scratching him under the chin, by serenading you with his deep, rich purr. A cat will still adore you on those days when you look your worst.

—PAM JOHNSON-BENNETT

Smitten

Have you ever been smitten by a kitten?
Don't lie.
It bounded up to you in its clumsy grace, all fuzz
and energy. . .uttered the slightest of meows. . .
looked up at you with all-knowing innocence. . .
and stole your heart.
Have you ever been smitten by a kitten?
Of course you have. Who hasn't?

Sleeping Cat Facts

The typical feline sleeps approximately sixteen hours a day, which means it spends about 60 percent of its life off-line. . . . Even in deepest slumber, a cat is still alert to its environment. The ears of a sleeping cat may twitch in response to sounds, and the slightest movement will instantly wake it.

—DAVID BRUNNER AND
SAM STALL

Pets or People?

Most pets display so many humanlike traits and emotions it's easy to forget they're not gifted with the English language and then get snubbed when we talk to them and they don't say anything back.

—STEPHENIE GEIST

A Cat's Prayer

Now I lay me down to sleep,
The king-size bed is soft and deep. . .
I sleep right in the center groove
My human can hardly move!

I've trapped her legs, she's tucked in tight
And here is where I pass the night
No one disturbs me or dares intrude
Till morning comes and "I want food!"

—UNKNOWN

Who Means the Most

When we honestly ask ourselves which person in our lives means the most to us, we often find that it is those who, instead of giving advice, solutions, or cures, have chosen rather to share our pain and touch our wounds with a warm and tender hand.

—HENRI NOUWEN

Hungry for More

It is impossible for a lover of cats to banish these alert, gentle, and discriminating little friends, who give us just enough of their regard and complaisance to make us hunger for more.

—AGNES REPPLIER

A Friend Who Cares

The friend who can be silent with us in a moment of despair or confusion, who can stay with us in an hour of grief and bereavement, who can tolerate not knowing,. not curing, not healing, . . .that is a friend who cares.

—HENRI NOUWEN

Remembering Bathsheba the Cat

Bathsheba! To whom none ever said scat —
No worthier cat
Ever sat on a mat
Or caught a rat.
Requiescat!

—JOHN GREENLEAF WHITTIER

A Spot of Sun
and a Lazy Cat

There was one spot of sun moving across the floor
as the day progressed. Leave it to the cat to find a
way to loll across the floor in that one spot of sun
until it disappeared into the dusk falling in the
room. No one loves a spot of sun like a lazy cat.

The Company He Keeps

A cat is a patient listener, even when you're telling a story for the third time. A cat is the most dependable alarm clock you'll ever have. A cat will show you how to enjoy life. A cat chooses the company he keeps.

—PAM JOHNSON-BENNETT

Precious

Following the 9/11 attacks, there were stories of amazing felines who survived against impossible odds. One of these was Precious, a cat who lived in a building that suffered terrible damage. Twenty days after the incident, rescuers discovered Precious on the roof of the damaged apartment building. Hungry and injured, she was thrilled to be reunited with her owners. Precious made a full recovery.

—ALLAN ZULLO AND
MARA BOYSON

Purring

The purr is at the heart of our close relationship
with the cat. However, there are few early historical
references to purring. One does occur in the
eulogy to Beland the cat, written by Joachim du
Bellay in the mid-sixteenth century: He was my
favorite plaything/And not forever purring/A long
and timeless/Grumbling litany.

—ROGER TABOR

If Cats Could Speak

If animals could speak, the dog would be a blundering outspoken fellow; but the cat would have the rare grace of never saying a word too much.

—MARK TWAIN

Fillet of Sol

The sun slants in, its light a wedge
Of carpet by the door.
And to that slice of sunlight
Goes my cat, now, to restore
Herself. This nap is therapeutic
(Like the tuna she devoured).
She seems to need this daily bask.
She thinks she's solar powered.

—LEE ANNY WYNN SNOOK

The Uncommon

Everything that is new or uncommon raises
a pleasure in the imagination, because it fills
the soul with an agreeable surprise, gratifies its
curiosity, and gives it an idea of which it was not
before possessed.

—JOSEPH ADDISON

Gifts from the Creator

The cat is the animal to whom the Creator gave
the biggest eye, the softest fur, the most supremely
delicate nostrils, a mobile ear, an unrivaled paw,
a curved claw, borrowed from a rose tree.

—COLETTE

A Curious Illusion

We tie bright ribbons around their necks,
and occasionally little tinkling bells, and we affect
to think that they are as sweet and vapid as the coy
name "kitty" by which we call them would imply.
It is a curious illusion. For, purring beside our
fireplaces and pattering along our back fences,
we have got a wild beast as uncowed and
uncorrupted as any under heaven.

—ALAN DEVOE

No Mistakes in Cat Land

In the human world, there is a thing called a
"mistake." There's no exact translation in the
feline language. . . . The concept is quite confusing
to cats since everything we do is done both
correctly and on purpose.

—JOE GARDEN

The Cost of a Kitten

The highest cost of the new kitten was not the
shredded curtains or the picked at furniture.
It wasn't the food or the vet visits or the toys that
multiplied like wild rabbits. No, the cost was the
hearts we gave away over and over again no matter
what she did or what the consequences were to us.

Unexpected Love

If you took a poll among cat owners,
an overwhelming number of them would tell you
that they hadn't been looking for a cat, hadn't
planned on one, and maybe didn't even care much
for cats—the feline love of their lives just walked
in. More often than not, it's the cats who
choose us.

—PAM JOHNSON-BENNETT

Thanks, Silly Friend

Thanks for the laughter you sent my way, silly friend. Thanks for your antics and sweetness. Thanks for your purring and nuzzly kisses. Thanks for the love that only you could have shown.

Forget Yourself

Develop interest in life as you see it; in people,
things, literature, music—the world is so rich,
simply throbbing with rich treasures, beautiful
souls and interesting people. Forget yourself.

—HENRY MILLER

The Honor of a Sparrow

I once had a sparrow alight upon my shoulder for a moment, while I was hoeing in a village garden, and I felt that I was more distinguished by that circumstance that I should have been by any epaulet I could have worn.

—HENRY DAVID THOREAU

Kilkenny Cats

There once were two cats of Kilkenny,
Each thought there was one cat too many;

So they fought and they fit,
And they scratched and they bit,

Till, excepting their nails
And the tips of their tails

Instead of two cats
There weren't any.

—IRISH LIMERICK

The Miracle of Forgiveness

Forgiveness is the answer to the child's dream of a miracle by which what is broken is made whole again, what is soiled is made clean again.

—DAG HAMMARSKJOLD

Rules and Rituals

Although all cat games have their rules and rituals, these vary with the individual player. The cat, of course, never breaks a rule. If it does not follow precedent, that simply means it has created a new rule and it is up to you to learn it quickly if you want the game to continue.

—SIDNEY DENHAM

Your Friend, But Not Your Slave

It is a matter to gain the affection of a cat. He is a philosophical animal, tenacious of his own habits, fond of order and neatness, and disinclined to extravagant sentiment. He will be your friend, if he finds you worthy of friendship, but not your slave. He keeps his free will though he loves, and will not do for you what he thinks unreasonable; but if he once gives himself to you, it is with absolute confidence and fidelity of affection.

—THEOPHILE GAUTIER

The Thing about Cats

The thing about cats as you might find,
Is that no one knows what they have in mind.
And I'll tell you something about that,
No one knows it less than my cat.

—JOHN CIARDI

We Belong Together

It's not that my cat is the prettiest cat, or the most well behaved or the sliest or shiest or most unusual. She has her eccentricities like any other cat and her difficulties like any other pet. The thing about my cat is this—that she's mine. Irrevocably. Without hesitation. Belonging to no other. That we belong together is one of the firmest realities of my life.

The Siamese Cat Song

We are Siamese if you please.
We are Siamese if you don't please.
Now we're looking over our new domisile,
If we like we stay for maybe quite a while.

—PEGGY LEE AND SONNY BURKE

A Lazy Dream

Are cats lazy? Well, more power to them if they
are. Which one of us has not entertained the
dream of doing just as he likes, when and how he
likes, and as much as he likes?

—DR. FERNAND MERY

Why cats?

Cats are the most popular pets in the United States, a fact which puzzles me immensely. Cats defy most of the normal rules about how and why animals came to enter the company of humans. A cat can be adaptive and perverse, affectionate and wary, gregarious and reclusive, independent and aloof. In spite of these paradoxes, I cannot imagine living without a cat.

—STEPHEN BUDIANSKY

The Danger of Unhappy Cats

When my cats aren't happy, I'm not happy.
Not because I care about their mood but because
I know they're just sitting there thinking up ways
to get even.

—PERCY BYSSHE SHELLEY

Nursery Rhyme

There was a crooked man,
   and he went a crooked mile
He found a crooked sixpence
   against a crooked stile
He bought a crooked cat,
   which caught a crooked mouse
And they all lived together
   in a little crooked house.

—NURSERY RHYME

When Have You Truly Lived?

You will find as you look back upon your life that the moments when you have truly lived are the moments when you have done things in the spirit of love.

—HENRY DRUMMOND

Feels Good, As It Should

Cats can be cooperative when something feels good, which, to a cat, is the way everything is supposed to feel as much of the time as possible.

—ROGER CARAS

Stimulating the Affection Gland

Apparently, through scientific research, it has been determined that a cat's affection gland is stimulated by snoring, thus explaining my cat's uncontrollable urge to rub against my face at 2 a.m.

—TERRI L. HANEY

What the Rabble Are Missing

It is easy to understand why the rabble dislike cats. A cat is beautiful; it suggests ideas of luxury, cleanliness, voluptuous pleasures.

—CHARLES BAUDELAIRE

The Most Beautiful Cat

I saw the most beautiful cat today. It was sitting by the side of the road, its two front feet neatly and graciously together. Then it gravely swished around its tail to completely and snugly encircle itself. It was so fit and beautifully neat, that gesture, and so self-satisfied —so complacent.

—ANNE MORROW LINDBERGH

See the Kitten on the Wall

See the kitten on the wall,
Sporting with the leaves that fall. . .

First at one, and then its fellow,
Just as light and just as yellow. . .

With a tiger-leap half-way
Now she meets the coming prey,

Lets it go as fast, and then
Has it in her power again. . . .

—WILLIAM WORDSWORTH

Cats Getting Fed

Cats are way above begging for food. Cats prefer the direct approach when it comes to getting our fair share—by being yowling, insufferable pests, or just hopping up and helping ourselves.

—JOE GARDEN

Once Burned. . .

We should be careful to get out of an experience only the wisdom that is in it—and stop there; lest we be like the cat that sits down on a hot stove lid. She will never sit down on a hot stove lid again—and that is well; but she will also never sit down on a cold one.

—MARK TWAIN

A Messy Subject

There is the little matter of disposal of droppings in which the cat is far ahead of its rivals. The dog is somehow thrilled by what he or any of his friends have produced, hates to leave it, adores smelling it, and sometimes eats it. . . . The cat covers it up if he can.

—PAUL GALLICO

Prayer for the Animals

Hear our prayer, Lord, for all animals,
May they be well-fed and well-trained and happy;
Protect them from hunger and fear and suffering;
And, we pray, protect specially, dear Lord,
The little cat who is the companion of our home,
Keep her safe as she goes abroad,
And bring her back to comfort us.

—AN OLD RUSSIAN PRAYER

The Key of Gratitude

Gratitude unlocks the fullness of life. It turns what
we have into enough, and more. It turns denial
into acceptance, chaos to order, confusion to
clarity. It can turn a meal into a feast, a house into
a home, a stranger into a friend. Gratitude makes
sense of our past, brings peace for today,
and creates a vision for tomorrow.

—MELODY BEATTIE

The Sad Absence of Purring

When you're used to hearing purring and suddenly it's gone, it's hard to silence the blaring sound of sadness.

—MISSY ALTIJD

He Restores My Soul

The LORD is my shepherd, I shall not be in want.
He makes me lie down in green pastures, he leads
me beside quiet waters, he restores my soul. He
guides me in paths of righteousness for his name's
sake.

—PSALM 23:1–3 NIV

Slow Down and Enjoy

Slow down and enjoy life. It's not only the scenery
you miss by going too fast—you also miss the
sense of where you are going and why.

—EDDIE CANTOR

Cats and Laundered Clothes

Is there anything as enticing to a young cat than a warm, clean basket of laundered clothes?
And he seems to prefer those that are a completely different color than he so that he can mark as many as possible with shedding fur.

The Unexplainable

Cats, with their shining eyes and silent footfalls, have always eluded explanation. Throughout the several thousand years of shared history between cats and human beings, cats have been a source of wonder and unease, reverence and superstition.

—STEPHEN BUDIANSKY

A Cat's Love

A cat's love may seem hard won at times, but oh, the sweetness of the unguarded feline heart which has been won over. It takes a certain amount of time and attention that creates the kind of safety that a kitty's heart revels in.

My Kitten

I have a little kitten with soft and shiny furr
And when I pet my kitten she goes purr, purr, purr.
Oh kitten, kitten, kitten, with soft and shiny furr
I love to pet my kitten and hear her purr, purr, purr.

—CHILDREN'S POEM FROM
CAT POEMS AND SONGS

The Nature of a Cat

The cat lives alone, has no need of society,
obeys only when she pleases, pretends to sleep that
she may see more clearly, and scratches everything
on which she can lay her paw.

—FRANÇOIS R. CHATEAUBRIAND

Cat Hair

Cat hair on the bedspread,
Cat hair on the chair.
Cat hair in the casserole,
Cat hair everywhere
Cat hair on my best coat,
Even on the mouse!
You live and eat and breathe cat hair,
When cats live in your house.

—UNKNOWN

The Sweetness of Solitude

When I dance, I dance; when I sleep, I sleep.
Nay, when I walk alone in a beautiful orchard, if
my thoughts are some part of the time taken up
with foreign occurrences, I some part of the time
call them back again to my walk, to the orchard, to
the sweetness of the solitude, and to myself.

—MICHEL DE MONTAIGNE

A Subtle Language

Cats speak a subtle language in which few sounds carry many meanings, depending on how they are sung or purred. "Mnrhnh" means comfortable soft chairs. It also means fish. It means genial companionship. . .and the absence of dogs.

—VAL SCHAFFNER

Rendezvous with a Shoe

No catnip tree
Could offer bliss
Of magnitude
To equal this
As in a transport
Of delight
My spaced-out cougar
Spends the night
His nose in cozy
Rendezvous
With my malodorous
Jogging shoe.

—DOROTHY HELLER

Cat or Dog?

My cat exhibits all kinds of behavior normally associated with dogs. He fetches and retrieves sticks, understands and reacts to commands, chases people and dogs down the street, and eats all sorts of things that cats shouldn't like. Do I have a cat? Or is he a dog in disguise?

A Cat's Type of Love

If the pull of the outside world is strong, there is also a pull towards the human. The cat may disappear on its own errands, but sooner or later, it returns once again for a little while, to greet us with its own type of love. Independent as they are, cats find more than pleasure in our company.

—LLOYD ALEXANDER

The Wildest Things

The beauty and fascination we find in cats are much the same as what we feel for the wildest things in nature, with the added fascination that these particular wild and beautiful things are willing to admit us to their world, even though they don't have any particular need to.

—STEPHEN BUDIANSKY

The Lessons of a Rollicking Good Time

Cats nurture, watch over, and play with us as if we were babes who didn't know how to take care of ourselves—and certainly didn't have a clue about when to indulge in a rollicking good time.

—ALLEN AND LINDA ANDERSON

Rooted Yet Apart

Cats were brought into human society by a
deliberate act of adventuresome and curious
human beings; there they grew to a critical mass
in a culture that in time came to venerate them
en masse; thence they spread wherever man went,
a vine circling the tree of humanity that always
planted its own roots nearby, yet apart.

—STEPHEN BUDIANSKY

The Soul of My Home—My Cat

I love cats because I love my home and after a while they become its visible soul.

—JEAN COCTEAU

Gentle Eyes

Gentle eyes that see so much,
Paws that have the quiet touch,
Purrs to signal "all is well"
And show more love than words could tell.
Graceful movements touched with pride,
A calming presence by our side.
A friendship that takes time to grow—
Small wonder why we love them so.

—UNKNOWN

Frugality and Happiness

Frugality is one of the most beautiful and joyful words in the English language, and yet one that we are culturally cut off from understanding and enjoying. The consumption society has made us feel that happiness lies in having things, and has failed to teach us the happiness of not having things.

—ELISE BOULDING

No Replacing a Cat

Another cat? Perhaps. For love there is also a
season; its seeds must be resown. But a family cat
is not replaceable like a worn-out coat or a set of
tires. Each new kitten becomes its own cat,
and none is repeated. I am four cats old,
measuring out my life in friends that have
succeeded but not replaced one another.

—IRVING TOWNSEND

Up on the Counter

Why then, if not to steal food, would a cat go up on the counter? Why did George Mallory try to go up on Mount Everest, which was quite a lot more trouble? Because it is there. Because of the view from the kitchen window. To lick the drips from the tap in the sink. To try to pry open the cupboards and see what's inside them, maybe to squeeze among the glassware. Or, on a rainy day, to look for small objects to knock onto the floor and see if they roll.

—BARBARA HOLLAND

To Share Your Life with a Cat

[Our cat] is ever close, ever present, ever observing but she rarely intrudes. Her world is linked to ours but does not revolve around it. To share your life with a cat is to see grace of body and spirit on a daily basis, if you pay attention, if you know what to look for.

—BRIAN KILCOMMONS
AND SARA WILSON

My Kitten Learned to Climb a Tree

My kitten learned to climb a tree so quickly and so easily, but he didn't learn to climb back down for weeks and weeks it seemed. Finally when I tired of lugging the ladder round to help him out, he found his way, and since that day he's climbed both up and down.

Chasing My Tail

I work and worry and chase a deadline, like a kitty after its own tail, until I wear myself out.
And usually it is then I realize that if I would just relax in the course of my efforts, not only would the list get done, but I would live more life in the midst of it.

The Soul of Breeding

Cats are admirable company. I am very fond of dogs, too; but their sphere is the field. In the house they do not understand that repose of manner which is the soul of breeding. The cat's manners or rather manner seems to have been perfected by generations, nay centuries, of familiar intercourse with the great and cultivated of the earth.

—ALGERNON S. LOGAN

Kindness, Beauty, and Truth

The ideals which have lighted my way, and time after time have given me new courage to face life cheerfully, have been Kindness, Beauty, and Truth. The trite subjects of human efforts, possessions, outward success, luxury have always seemed to me contemptible.

—ALBERT EINSTEIN

Why Cats Groom

Cats are the ultimate narcissists. You can tell this by all the time they spend on personal grooming. Dogs aren't like this. A dog's idea of personal grooming is to roll in a dead fish.

—JAMES GORMAN

I Love My Little Kitty

I love my little kitty
Her coat is so warm.
And if I don't hurt her
She'll do me no harm.
I won't pull her tail,
Or drive her away
And kitty and I
Very gently will play.

—MOTHER GOOSE

The Point in Life

The point in life is to know what's enough—why
envy those otherworld immortals? With the
happiness held in one inch-square heart you can
fill the whole space between heaven and earth.

—GENSEI

A Cure for Tension

You cannot look at a sleeping cat and feel tense.

—JANE PAULEY

Deadly Fascination

I will admit to feeling exceedingly proud when any cat has singled me out for notice; for, of course, every cat is really the most beautiful woman in the room. That is part of their deadly fascination.

—E. V. LUCAS

A Territorial Nature

The dog is a pack animal. He hunts in a pack
and his whole social structure is built on the pack
mentality. A cat, on the other hand, is a sociable
animal but not the pack animal that a dog is. His
social structure is built upon his sense of territory.

—PAM JOHNSON-BENNETT

Saying Good-bye

We said good-bye to our old friend, the feline
equivalent of the kids' nanny and playmate.
We said good-bye because he was old and tired and
it was time for him to go. And we cried together,
but sent him on the way with our gratitude and
love and all the warmth in our hearts.

Captain, the Soul Mate

My soul mate was Captain. Together we caught frogs, climbed trees, hid from my brothers—we were a team. No one had ever told us the lie that cats are aloof, independent, or uncaring. Captain certainly never was. He comforted me when I was lonely, I cuddled him when he was. He was an incorruptibly fine soul, and I am the richer to have known him.

—SARA WILSON

I Choose You

We can feel lonely with lots of others around. We may feel "not okay." It is easy to give up hope. We need to hear a voice that says, "I choose you." And the touch of a finger—or a paw—means so much.

—MARTA FELBER

Love or Hate?

It is curious that 17 percent of Americans express a dislike of cats, yet cats have since the 1980s surpassed dogs as the most popular pet in the United States. Our love/hate relationship with cats does not limit their prevalence.

—STEPHEN BUDIANSKY

A Poet's Cat

A Poet's Cat, sedate and grave
As poet well could wish to have,
Was much addicted to inquire
For nooks to which she might retire,
And where, secure as mouse in chink,
She might repose, or sit and think.

—WILLIAM COWPER

Training Your Human

Training your human is a thankless task.
"Why bother with it?" some kittens may ask.
The fate of the world is the issue at hand,
As felines worldwide stake a claim for their land.
Make no bones about it, we cats own the joint.
We spray in the corners to drive home the point.

—UNKNOWN

The Rewards of the Simple Life

To find the universal elements enough; to find the air and the water exhilarating; to be refreshed by a morning walk or an evening saunter. . .to be thrilled by the stars at night; to be elated over a bird's nest or a wildflower in spring—these are some of the rewards of the simple life.

—JOHN BURROUGHS

My Cat the Editor

If by chance I seated myself to write, she very slyly, very tenderly, seeking protection and caresses, would softly take her place on my knee and follow the comings and goings of my pen—sometimes effacing, with an unintentional stroke of her paw, lines of whose tenor she disapproved.

—PIERRE LOTI

A Special Friend

A cat is a very special friend who comes into your life. When it comes it brings warmth, companionship, contentment, and love. Whether it's long-haired, short-haired, pedigreed or "Heinz" makes no difference. A cat, though independent, has a way of letting you know that without you life just wouldn't be worthwhile.

—SHARON LUNDBLAD

I Am a Cat

I am a cat. As yet I have no name. I have no idea where I was born. All I remember is that I was miawing in a dampish dark place when, for the first time, I saw a human being.

—SOSEKI NATSUME, AIKO ITO

The Sleepingest Cats

The simplest pleasures of life are the quietest
moments, the sleepingest cats, the gentlest of
winds, the lightest of rains, the tenderest of smiles,
the most lingering touches. These are the things
that remain in our hearts and offer us strength
when the world crashes in.

Most Unusual Cat Names

Veterinary Pet Insurance Company, a provider of
pet health insurance, recently published the ten
most unusual cat names for 2009. These included
Snag L. Tooth, Velvet Elvis, Blue Man Chew,
Thurston Picklesworth III, and Polly Prissypants.
Pet owners insisted that these names were perfect
for their particular felines.

—VETERINARY PET INSURANCE
COMPANY

Don't Pass Me By

I can rarely remember having passed a cat in the street without stopping to speak to it.

—BRUCE MARSHALL

The Right to Be a Cat

The things which man gives to him are not so
precious or essential that he will trade them for his
birth-right, which is the right to be himself—
a furred four-footed being of ancient lineage,
loving silence and aloneness and the night,
and esteeming the smell of rat's blood above any
possible human excellence.

—ALAN DEVOE

Here's What I Do

I purr and your blues fade away.
I snuggle close and a frown turns to a smile.
I play chase and your world fills with laughter.
And in return, all I ask, is two meals a day. . .
and all your love.

—STUART AND
LINDA MACFARLANE

Only a Cat

I'm only a cat,
and I stay in my place. . .
Up there on your chair,
on your bed or your face!

I'm only a cat,
and I don't finick much. . .
I'm happy with cream
and anchovies and such!

I'm only a cat,
and we'll get along fine. . .
As long as you know
I'm not yours. . .you're all mine!

—UNKNOWN

This Earthly Happiness

Good heavens, of what uncostly material is our earthly happiness composed—if we only knew it! What incomes have we not had from a flower, and how unfailing are the dividends of the seasons!

—JAMES RUSSELL LOWELL

How to Recognize a Cat Lover

Cat lovers can readily be identified. Their clothes always look old and well used. Their sheets look like bath towels and their bath towels look like a collection of knitting mistakes.

—ERIC GURNEY

Unfailing Love

May your unfailing love be my comfort, according
to your promise to your servant.
Let your compassion come to me that I may live,
for your law is my delight.

—PSALM 119:76–77 NIV

True Happiness

True happiness is of a retired nature, and an enemy to pomp and noise; it arises, in the first place, from the enjoyment of one's self, and in the next from the friendship and conversation of a few select companions.

—JOSEPH ADDISON

Sleeping Cats

Perhaps the most striking expression of love between cats occurs when they are relaxing or sleeping. It is in these moments of total intimacy, nestled together tight as can be, drowsing tranquilly, that they become one.

—HANS WALTER SILVESTER

Kitty Corner

Over on Cannery Row, the Kitty Corner was a swinging, jumping, happening place. On Saturday night everybody was there, laughing and singing and dancing and flirting, playing cards and just hanging with the gang. But Miss Kitty, the proprietor, didn't tolerate any misbehavior. Get rowdy, and with a mere nod to Bart the Bouncer, she'd have you thrown out on your whiskers.

You Do Not Win My Heart

You loved me when the fire was warm,
But, now I stretch a fondling arm,
You eye me and depart.
Cold eyes, sleek skin, and velvet paws,
You win my indolent applause,
You do not win my heart!

—A.C. BENSON

Well-Trained

I never cease to be amazed by how incredibly clever and manipulative the average pet cat can be. It is rather humbling and intensely amusing to think that we can be so successfully trained by a small furry creature. Cats are supposedly well beneath us on the evolutionary scale, but sometimes I wonder.

—VICKY HALLS

A Matter of Health and Hygiene

A cat licking herself solves most of the problems of infection. We wash too much and finally it kills us.

—WILLIAM CARLOS WILLIAMS

Cat Wishes

He blinks upon the hearth-rug,
And yawns in deep content,
Accepting all the comforts
That Providence has sent. . .

Life will go on forever,
With all that cat can wish;
Warmth, and the glad procession
Of fish and milk and fish.

Only—the thought disturbs him—
He's noticed once or twice,
That times are somehow breeding
A nimbler race of mice.

—SIR ALEXANDER GRAY

Invite Simplicity In

You can't force simplicity; but you can invite
it in by finding as much richness as possible in
the few things at hand. Simplicity doesn't mean
meagerness but rather a certain kind of richness,
the fullness that appears when we stop stuffing the
world with things.

—THOMAS MOORE

Hidden Dramas

Do you see that kitten chasing so prettily her own tail? If you could look with her eyes, you might see her surrounded with hundreds of figures performing complex dramas, with tragic and comic issues, long conversations, many characters, many ups and downs of fate.

—RALPH WALDO EMERSON

De-stressor

If you're lucky enough to own a cat consider
yourself one of life's winners because when you
have a cat around you'll never be lonely; the sound
of its purr will give you comfort, and as you hold it
and pet it, stress will slip away.

—SHARON LUNDBLAD

Cats and Their People

Communication and understanding are the two
most important links between cats and their
owners. It is obvious to sensitive and caring owners
that their cats are aware when the owners are
unhappy or in ill health. Likewise, the cats respond
with joyful play when the owner's mood is jolly.

—ANITRA FRAZIER AND
NORMA ECKROATE

To Be Like My Cat

I wish I had the contentment of my kitty who, while industrious in his own way, understands the importance of taking a nap or curling up beside someone important to him or enjoying a spot of sun on the floor before it moves on with the day.

Cat Dialect

Cats communicate using body posture, movement, voice, and scent. Their language is universal. A cat from Greece will understand a cat from Canada perfectly. Seemingly, no cat speaks with an accent.

—BRIAN KILCOMMONS AND
SARAH WILSON

Fear of Felines

Alexander the Great, Napoleon, and Hitler. . .
were apparently terrified of small felines. . . . If you
want to conquer the world you had better not share
even a moment with an animal that refuses to be
conquered at any price, by anyone.

—DESMOND MORRIS

Would You Come Out?

There's a mouse house
In the hall wall
With a small door
By the hall floor
Where the fat cat
Sits all day,
Sits that way
All day
Every day
Just to say
"Come out and play."

To the nice mice
In the mouse house
In the hall wall
With the small door
By the hall floor.

—JOHN CIARDI

Cats and Intellectuals

Cats are the natural companions of intellectuals.
They are silent watchers of dreams, inspiration,
and patient research.

—DR. FERNAND MERY

Striking a Pose

It seems like my cat can make time stand still when
he strikes a pose and focuses on some unseen point
and stares for all he's worth. Sometimes I hold my
breath just to feel the peace in the moment,
the peace that he in his stillness affords me.

To Live Content with Small Means

To live content with small means; to seek elegance rather than luxury, and refinement rather than fashion; to be worthy, not respectable, and wealthy, not rich; to listen to stars and birds, babes and sages, with open heart; to study hard; to think quietly, act frankly, talk gently, , await occasions, hurry never; in a word, tolet the spiritual, unbidden and unconscious, grow up through the common— this is my symphony.

—WILLIAM HENRY CHANNING

Can't Do a Thing with This Hair

I don't think it is so much the actual bath that most cats dislike; I think it's the fact that they have to spend a good part of the day putting their hair back in place.

—DEBBIE PETERSON

A Curious Effect

Cats have a curious effect on people. They seem to excite more extreme sentiments than any other animals. There are people who cannot remain in the room with a cat—who feel instinctively the presence of a cat even though they do not actually see it. On the other hand, there are people who, whatever they may be doing, will at once get up and fondle a cat immediately [when] they see it.

—ARTHUR PONSONBY

The Language of the Tail

The carriage of the tail is often a clue to how your cat is feeling. A tail held high is jaunty, enthusiastic, or playful. A tail between the legs or wrapped very tightly around the angles indicates fear. . . A cat uses his tail for balance when he leaps. He can also use it to control nervousness and excitement by swinging or lashing the tail as an outlet for tension or to drain off excess energy.

—ANITRA FRAZIER AND
NORMA ECKROATE

Defining Simple Moments

My definition of simple things has changed over the years, and a lot of those changes have come from the feline family members we have taken into our home, those who can stretch a moment out further than I ever imagined. It seems with cats, as independent as they can be, they still lavish moments of togetherness. They gather where the family is and simply let time pass right by. I've learned so much from them.

Who Owns Whom?

Do you watch bad TV shows because your cat is sitting on the remote? Do you put off making the bed until the cat gets up? Does your cat sleep on your head? Do you scoop out the litter box after each use? Do you wait at the litter box with the scoop in your hand?

—UNKNOWN

Sitting Pretty

Even overweight cats instinctively know the cardinal rule: When fat, arrange yourself in slim poses.

—JOHN WEITZ

Any Good I Can Do

I expect to pass through this world but once;
any good thing therefore that I can do, or any
kindness that I can show to any fellow creature,
let me do it now; let me not defer or neglect it,
for I shall not pass this way again.

—ETTIENE DE GRELLET

Five O'clock Tea

When the tea is brought at five o'clock,
And all the neat curtains are drawn with care,
The little black cat with bright green eyes
Is suddenly purring there.

—HAROLD MONRO

St. Jerome's Cat

St. Jerome in his study kept a great big cat,
It's always in his pictures, with its feet upon the mat.
Did he give it milk to drink, in a little dish?
When it came to Friday's, did he give it fish?
If I lost my little cat, I'd be sad without it;
I should ask St. Jeremy what to do about it.

—TRADITIONAL ENGLISH
NURSERY RHYME

Material Things

The world has to learn that the actual pleasure derived from material things is of rather low quality on the whole and less even in quantity than it looks to those who have not tried it.

—OLIVER WENDELL HOLMES

A Purring Alarm Clock

The best kind of alarm clock is the purring kind.

—ALEXIS F. HOPE

Watch a Cat

Watch a cat when it enters a room for the first time. It searches and smells about, it is not quiet for a moment, it trusts nothing until it has examined and made acquaintance with everything.

—JEAN-JACQUES ROUSSEAU

The Difference between Cats and Dogs

There's a joke about cats and dogs that conveys their differences perfectly. A dog says, "You pet me, you feed me, you shelter me, you love me, you must be God." A cat says, "You pet me, you feed me, you shelter me, you love me, I must be God."

—BOB SJOGREN AND
GERALD ROBISON

Touching Someone You Love

Stroking the back of my cat is the most calming experience of my day. In fact, I am sure at times that she comes to me for a good rub not for her benefit at all, but so that I can remember for a moment the simple joy and ultimate benefit of touching someone I love.

How Did This Happen?

Within minutes of his arrival the new kitten has endeared himself to everyone. By the time he is one year old he rejects all but the most expensive cat food and commandeers the best chair in the living room. On his tenth birthday he has the master bed almost entirely to himself.

—VICKY HALLS

The Cat Mourned

Pet was never mourned as you,
Purrer of the spotless hue,
Plumy tail, and wistful gaze
While you humoured our queer ways. . .
Never another pet for me!
Let your place all vacant be

—THOMAS HARDY

High Self-Sufficiency Is Her Charm

A cat cares for you only as a source of food, security, and a place in the sun. Her high self-sufficiency is her charm.

—CHARLES HORTON COOLEY

Smile for the Camera

Cats make exquisite photographs. . . . They don't
keep bouncing at you to be kissed, just as you get
the lens adjusted.

—GLADYS TABER

Cats Sleep Anywhere

Cats sleep anywhere, any table, any chair.
Top of piano, window-ledge, in the middle, on the
edge. Open draw, empty shoe, anybody's lap will
do. Fitted in a cardboard box, in the cupboard with
your frocks. Anywhere! They don't care!
Cats sleep anywhere.

—ELEANOR FARJEON

The Best Things in Life

The best things in life are nearest: Breath in your nostrils, light in your eyes, flowers at your feet, duties at your hand, the path of right just before you. Then do not grasp at the stars, but do life's plain, common work as it comes, certain that daily duties and daily bread are the sweetest things in life.

—ROBERT LOUIS STEVENSON

A Lion in a Jungle

A cat is a lion in a jungle of small bushes.

—INDIAN PROVERB

A Computer Is like a Cat?

A computer and a cat are somewhat alike—they both purr, and like to be stroked, and spend a lot of the day motionless. They also have secrets they don't necessarily share.

—JOHN UPDIKE

Cats and Humans

A cat's got her own opinion of human beings.
She don't say much, but you can tell enough to
make you anxious not to hear the whole of it.

—JEROME K. JEROME

A Matter of Perspective

I have just been given a very engaging Persian
kitten, named after St. Philip Neri (who was very
sound on cats) and his opinion is that I have been
given to him.

—EVELYN UNDERHILL

Caressing the Tiger

God made the cat in order that man might have the pleasure of caressing the tiger.

—DR. FERNAND MERY

Life Lessons

I have learned a lot from my cat. When life is loud and scary, go under the bed and nap. When you want someone to notice you, sit on the book that person is reading. And if someone sits in your chair, glare at her until she moves.

Comparing People and Animals

I have been studying the traits and dispositions of the "lower animals" (so called) and contrasting them with the traits and dispositions of man. I find the result humiliating to me.

—MARK TWAIN

Pussy-cat, Pussy-cat

"Pussy-cat, pussy-cat, where have you been?"
"I've been to London to look at the Queen."
"Pussy-cat, pussy-cat, what did you there?"
"I frightened a little mouse under the chair."

—MOTHER GOOSE

Black-Cat Luck

A cat as black
As blackest coal
Is out upon
His midnight stroll,
His steps are soft,
His walk is slow,
His eyes are gold,
They flash and glow.
And so I run
And so I duck,
I do not need
His black-cat luck.

—UNKNOWN

Delight in the Simple Things

Teach us delight in the simple things,
And mirth that has no bitter springs;
Forgiveness free of evil done,
And love to all men beneath the sun.

—RUDYARD KIPLING

A Wee Ball o' Fur

Who would believe such pleasure from a wee ball o' fur?

—IRISH SAYING

Seek Peace

Does anyone want to live a life
   that is long and prosperous?
Then keep your tongue from speaking evil
   and your lips from telling lies!
Turn away from evil and do good.
   Search for peace, and work to maintain it.

—PSALM 34:12–14 NLT

Look Deeper

Do not judge men by mere appearances; for the
light laughter that bubbles on the lip often mantles
over the depths of sadness, and the serious look
may be the sober veil that covers a divine peace
and joy.

—EDWARD CHAPIN

Here's to the Feline

Here's to the feline with her fur and her eyes and her beautiful nose, her ears, and her paws, and her tail in the air, her friendship and peace and her calming stare. Here's to the the feline who walks on me, plays with my hand like it's her personal toy and sleeps on my face when given the chance. What a joy to share my life with her.

My Cat

My cat rubs my leg and starts to purr with a soft
little rumble, a soft little whirr, as if she had
motors inside of her.

I say, "Nice Kitty," and stroke her fur,
and though she can't talk and I can't purr,
she understands me, and I do her.

—AILEEN FISHER

Moggies

America, which has made an art form of slang, does not seem to have an accepted word for the non-pedigree cat, the "average Joe" of the cat world. Terms used such as alley cat, common cat, and tabby all have other meanings. The British call all non-purebred cats "moggies," a word worth introducing to Americans.

—ROGER TABOR

Cat Eyes

Eyes are indeed the window to the soul, especially with cats. Cats, not being a deceiving group, will let you know precisely what they think of you with a glance.

—BRIAN KILCOMMONS
AND SARAH WILSON

Cats Lying Down

A cat pours his body on the floor like water.

—WILLIAM LYON PHELPS

Special Indeed

When you're special to a cat, you're special indeed. . .she brings to you the gift of her preference of you, the sight of you, the sound of your voice, the touch of your hand.

—LEONORE FLEISHER

What Makes Life Worthwhile?

It is the simple things of life that make living worthwhile, the sweet fundamental things such as love and duty, work and rest, and living close to nature. There are not hothouse blossoms that can compare in beauty and fragrance with my bouquet of wildflowers.

—LAURA INGALLS WILDER

On Its Own Terms

One must love a cat on its own terms.

—PAUL GRAY

Here's Lies a Pretty Cat

Here lies a pretty cat:
Its mistress, who never loved anyone,
Loved it madly;
Why bother to say so?
Everyone can see it.

—EPITAPH ON TOMBSTONE
OF CAT

The Power of a Sleeping Cat

A sleeping cat in a room has the effect of nothing short of a lit candle. It is a carrier of peace, an agent of quiet. And should that cat stretch full-length from paw to tail, its influence is only heightened.

Cats and Dogs

I love my dogs, don't get me wrong. They come
when I call and they love me no matter what.
But my cat has a special place in my heart as well.
She holds herself separate at times, but not for the
sake of game-playing or holding out. She is simply
being true to herself, and, soon enough, I know
she'll be by my side secretly rolling her eyes at the
big canine galoots with whom we share our home.

The Miracle of Me, by Bubba

I know I was designed to be
Adored by all who encounter me
With glossy fur and emerald eyes
My glory's sure to mesmerize.
Those hapless humans who think that
A dog's a dog; a cat's a cat
Will surely come around to see
The miracle that is me.

—FRANNY SYUFY

The Litter Box

The litter box proves that cats are passive-aggressive. As soon as I clean it, my cat Lucy immediately has the urge to use it.

When important company comes, she digs and scratches her litter until the room is filled with uncomfortable silence. And if she thinks it is too full, she empties it on the floor.

Delicacy and Reserve

All cats and kittens, whether royal Persians or of
the lowliest estate, resent patronage, jocoseness
(which they rightly hold to be in bad taste),
and demonstrative affection,—those lavish
embraces which lack delicacy and reserve.

—AGNES REPPLIER

Mother Teresa on Animals

They, too, are created by the same loving hand of God which Created us. . . . It is our duty to protect them and to promote their well-being.

—MOTHER TERESA

Dickens's Cat

Charles Dickens's cat give birth to a litter of cats. Dickens only allowed one of these kittens to remain with its mother. The kitten was known as the "Master's Cat." The kitten would snuff out Dickens's candle in order to gain his attention.

The Most Valuable Things in Life

The most valuable things in life are not measured in monetary terms. The really important things are not houses and lands, stocks and bonds, automobiles and real estate, but friendships, trust, confidence, empathy, mercy, love and faith.

—BERTRAND RUSSELL

The Most Irresistible Comedian

A kitten is the most irresistible comedian in the world. Its wide-open eyes gleam with wonder and mirth. It darts madly at nothing at all, and then, as though suddenly checked in the pursuit, prances sideways on its hind legs with ridiculous agility and zeal.

—AGNES REPPLIER

Outside and Inside

Outside of a cat, a book is man's best friend.
Inside of a cat, it's too dark to read.

—SIGN AT LILAC HEDGE
    BOOKSHOP, NORWICH, VT

An Embarrassment

It was [my cat's] firm belief that I had the power to turn off the rain, brush away the clouds, make the sun come back to shine upon the window ledge, modify the temperature, (and) perform other miracles as required. I found my failure to live up to his high esteem somewhat embarrassing.

—ERA ZISTEL

Walk, Schmalk

Now a cat will not take an excursion merely because a man wants a walking companion. Walking is a human habit into which dogs readily fall but it is a distasteful form of exercise to a cat unless he has a purpose in view.

—CARL VAN VECHTEN

DAY 348

A Selfless, Shellfish Indulgence

I shall never forget the indulgence with which
Dr. Johnson treated Hodge, his cat, for whom he
himself used to go out and buy oysters, lest the
servants, having that trouble, should take a dislike
to the poor creature.

—JAMES BOSWELL

Catlike

Soft and sensuous are descriptive words that can
be applied as equally to a cat as to a woman.
One of Aesop's fables tells how a man fell in love
with his cat, which Venus, in compassion, changed
into a beautiful woman; however, when a mouse
ran by their bed, she leaped out onto it, changing
back into a cat.

—ROGER TABOR

Kindness

Guard well within yourself that treasure, kindness.
Know how to give without hesitation, how to lose
without regret, how to acquire without meanness.

—GEORGE SAND

Religion, Animals, and our Perpetual Responsibility

Personally, I would not give a fig for any man's religion whose horse, cat, and dog do not feel its benefits. Life in any form is our perpetual responsibility.

—S. PARKES CADMAN

Albert and Sizi

Although left-handed, Dr. Schweitzer would often write prescriptions with his right hand because his cat Sizi liked to sleep on his left arm and could not be disturbed.

True Contentment

True contentment is a thing as active as agriculture. It is the power of getting out of any situation all that there is in it. It is arduous and it is rare.

—GILBERT KEITH CHESTERTON

A Cat's Perfect Plaything

Of all the toys available, none is better designed
than the owner himself. A large multipurpose
plaything, its parts can be made to move in almost
any direction. It comes completely assembled,
and it makes a sound when you jump on it.

—STEPHEN BAKER

Caesar

There was an old bulldog named Caesar,
Who went for a cat just to tease her;
But she spat and she spit,
Till the old bulldog quit.
Now when poor Caesar sees her, he flees her.

—UNKNOWN

The Comfort of a Furry Face

The comfort of a furry face against my cheek is a value without measure. The simplicity of the moment, the generosity of the gesture, softens the edges of the world, and brings me to a quieter place.

I Gave My Cat a Bath

I gave my cat a bath once. I thought she'd feel
so much better. But in the end, we were both the
worse for it and I've never done it to either of us
since. Though I have to admit that every so often
we find ourselves in the bathroom at the same
time, and I feel sure we both remember the horror.

Disney Cats

Over the years, Disney films have capitalized on our love for cats. At least fifteen Disney movies have central characters that are felines! These include *The Three Lives of Thomasina*, *Pinocchio*, *Lady and the Tramp*, *The Aristocats*, and *The Cat From Outer Space*.

Scratching Post

My cat has a theory about the scratching post. In a nutshell, it is, "Do not use it." When she passes the post, she looks at it with disdain and sticks her tail in the air. Then, with an air of entitlement, she scratches the doorframe. Satisfied, she wanders off to take yet another nap.

Cats

They stand at the door.
Two sets of golden eyes, staring into the darkness.
Ears twitching,
Tail tips curled loosely.
Whiskers at attention.
They stand, peering out at the night, scenting.
Out the door!
Gone, vanished into the shadows!
Dead mice on my doorstep in the morning.
A present.

—CRYSTAL WIZARD

The Unawakened Soul

Until one has loved an animal, a part of one's soul
remains unawakened.

—ANATOLE FRANCE

Old Possum's Book of Practical Cats

The Nobel Prize-winning British poet, playwright, and cat lover, T. S. Eliot, wrote an entire book of poems about cats. His *Old Possum's Book of Practical Cats* was set to music by Andrew Lloyd Weber and became the long-running musical, *Cats*.

The Glory of Friendship

The glory of friendship is not the outstretched hand, nor the kindly smile, nor the joy of companionship; it's the spiritual inspiration that comes to one when he discovers that someone else believes in him and is willing to trust him with his friendship.

—RALPH WALDO EMERSON

The Cat and the Moon

The cat has always been associated with the moon.
Like the moon it comes to life at night, escaping
from humanity and wandering over housetops with
its eyes beaming out through the darkness.

—PATRICIA DALE-GREEN

A Cat Blessing

May there always be a cat to comfort you when you are sad, to amuse you when you are bored, to keep you company when you are lonely, to remind you that a nap in the sun is a fine thing, and to show you that the natural world is always just a purr and a pounce away.

—BRIAN KILCOMMONS
AND SARA WILSON

Notes